# This Annoying Life

## A Mindless Coloring Book
## for the Highly Stressed

*by* Oslo Davis

CHRONICLE BOOKS

SAN FRANCISCO

*This book is for Minami and Yuna,*
*My very unannoying daughters.*

First published in the United States in 2016 by Chronicle
Books LLC.

The contents of this book were published in Australia in
2015 and 2016 by Black Inc. under the titles *This Annoying
Life* and *This Annoying Domestic Life*. Copyright © 2015,
2016 by Oslo Davis. All rights reserved. No part of this
book may be reproduced in any form without written
permission from the publisher.

ISBN: 978-1-4521-5978-2

Manufactured in China

Cover design and illustrations by Oslo Davis
Designed by Michael Morris

10 9 8 7 6 5 4

Chronicle Books LLC
680 Second Street
San Francisco, CA 94107
www.chroniclebooks.com

Chronicle books and gifts are available at special quantity discounts
to corporations, professional associations, literacy programs,
and other organizations. For details and discount information,
please contact our premiums department at corporatesales@
chroniclebooks.com or at 1-800-759-0190.

# Introduction

First of all, let me say there are many wonderful things in life, like the laughter of children, a puppy tripping over its paws, or a porpoise balancing a ball on its snout. But we all know there's still lots of annoying stuff.

And I'm not talking about the big annoying stuff, like death, widespread misery etc., but the small stuff that we all sweat every day, the minor disturbances that ruin everything.

Like when the grocery bag rips. The ice cube trays are completely empty. You accidently knock over a row of bicycles. The bookshelf collapses. Something horrible leaks in the fridge. The toaster catches fire. Your colored pencil breaks. . . .

We hate this stuff, especially when it happens to us. As a remedy, this book invites you to color your cares away, to feel a little thrill of schadenfreude in seeing other people get annoyed, and to open a path to calm, to mindfulness (whatever that means).

In conclusion, I'd like to misappropriate a quote by Thich Nhat Hanh, the author of *Peace Is Every Step: The Path of Mindfulness in Everyday Life*, who famously said "Walk as if you are kissing the earth with your feet," by saying "Color in as if you are kissing this annoying life with your pencils." There, doesn't that feel better?

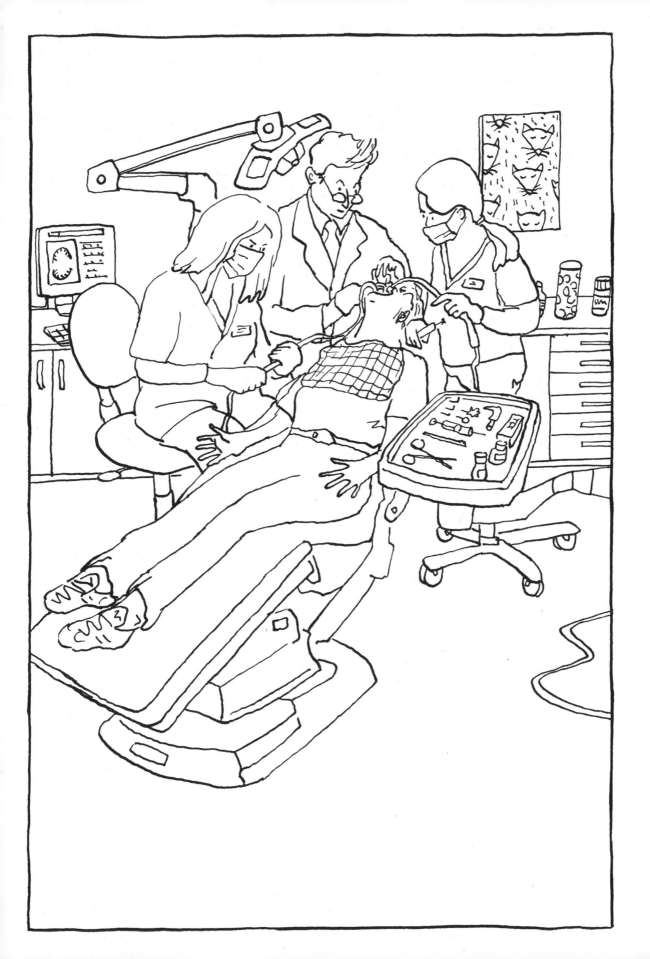

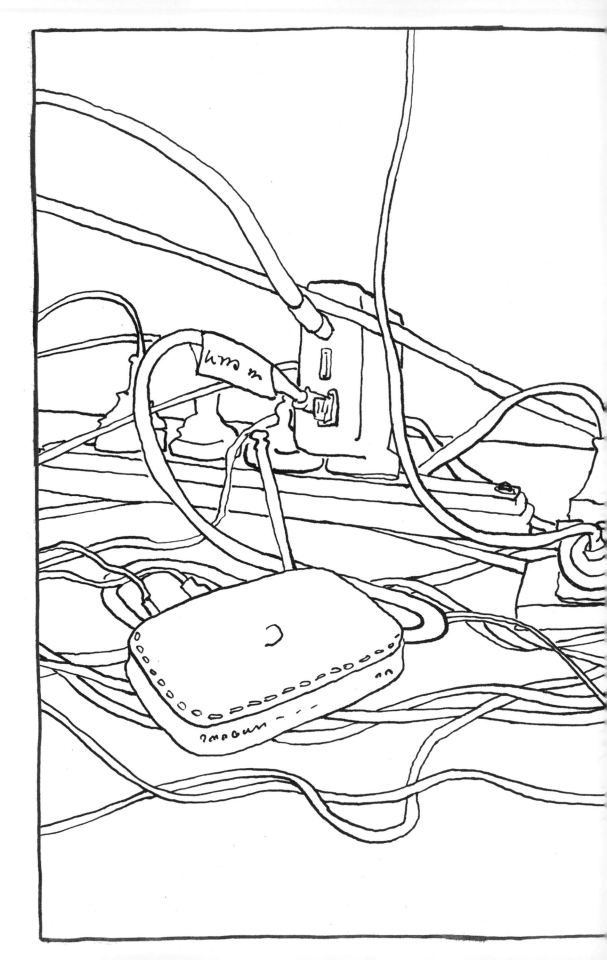

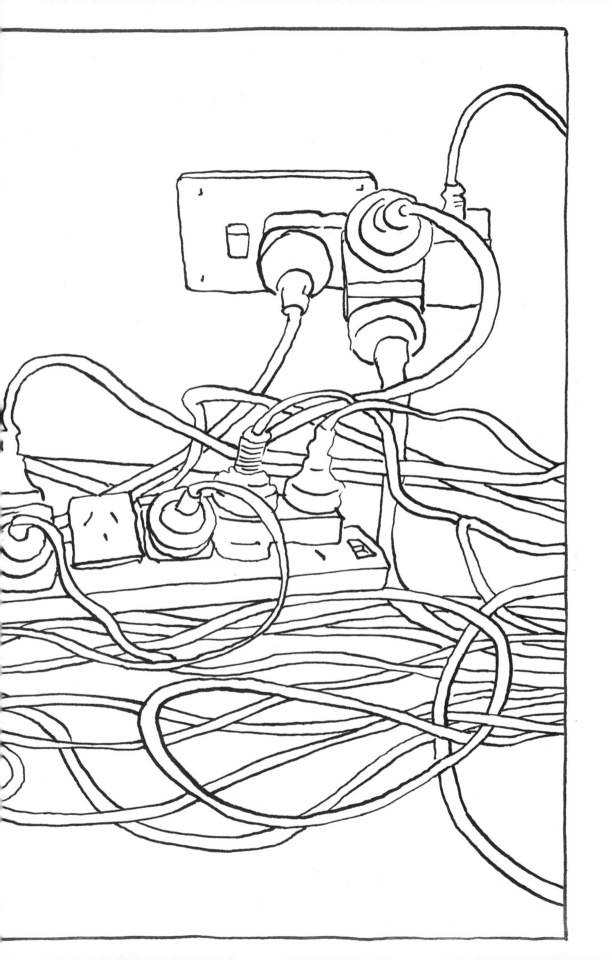

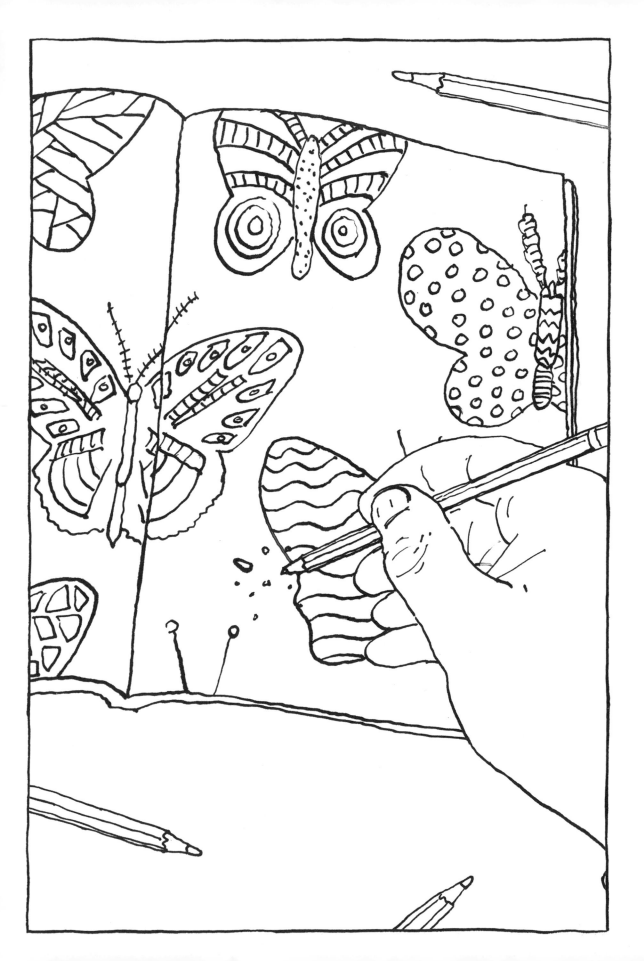

3:45 AM

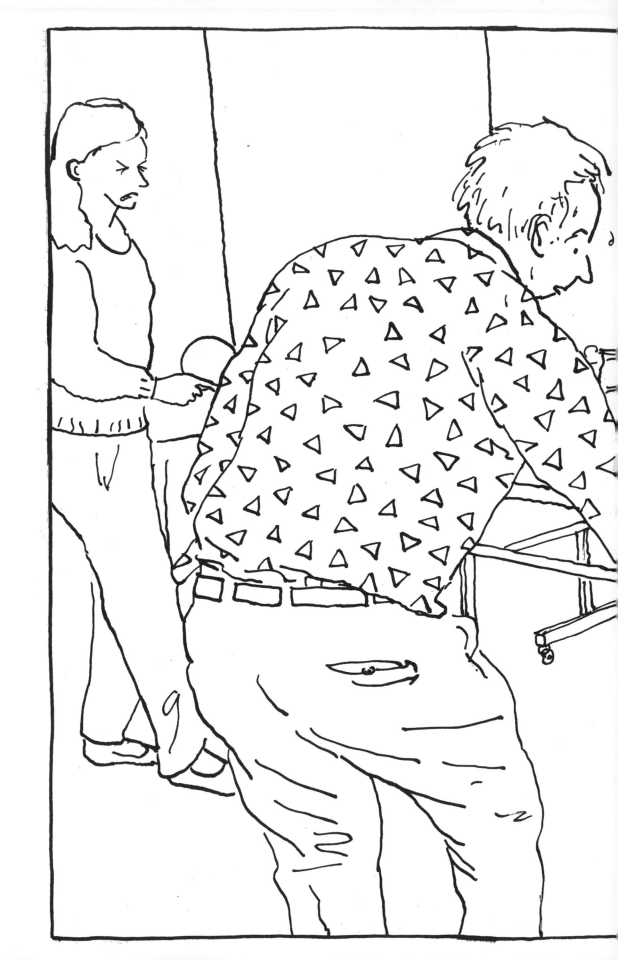